# Demolition Fedora

Also by Vernon Frazer

POETRY

*Free Fall* (Potes & Poets 1999)
*Sing Me One Song of Evolution* (Beneath the Underground 1998)
*Demon Dance* (Nude Beach 1995)
*A Slick Set of Wheels* (Water Row 1987)

FICTION

*Stay Tuned to This Channel* (Beneath the Underground 1999)

RECORDINGS

*Song of Baobab* (VFCI 1997)
*Slam!* (Woodcrest 1991)
*Sex Queen of the Berlin Turnpike* (Woodcrest 1988)

# Demolition Fedora

by

Vernon Frazer

Potes & Poets Press Inc
Elmwood CT
2000

ACKNOWLEDGMENTS

Some of the poems in this collection first appeared in
*POTEPOETZINE*, *Peaky Hide* and *ZYX*.

First Edition



ISBN 1-893541-23-1

Cover Art: Carol Ganick

Potes & Poets Press Inc
181 Edgemont Avenue
Elmwood CT 06110-1005

Printed in the United States of America

*To S. Michael DeRosa*
*for a lifetime of friendship*

## Admirable Constraint

the pentecostal fury of lemmings
knows no tell-tale badger's libido

limited though it might seem
to the unannointed masters of destiny
drenched in penny-pinching flurries
of modular polarity

their clandestine stentors tense
the silence about blatant nodules

as rumor, as theory, as truth
transcends the furry unknown
whose pastors recite chapters perverse
to primate storage stations

safely rations currency
of the hybrids in their midst

## After the Hanging

pontifical encomiums ensue
the weary stuffed eerie harmonies in picture frames
where the mirror lies

intersection bids
the dance of inert palettes pirouettes
the vision tricyclic

wheels skid farewell
to dainty wind chimes dancing
concerts of air

wherever the motion
lies flat or sharp the same temper
frames its dis-

lines accrue
graphs skew their charteng
impugn its spin

wall hangings
synaptic to the gallery's spread
of dips

chip the mode
its nodule dips then leaps
canvas tents

in miniature
spread the lunges of breath looking
eye to eye

politely speak
sensory modes shifting neuroleptic
transmissions

leaping across
the rumor's suicidal drawbridge
lifts medium

## A Lessoning of History

hung sung duet offset the coker's snore
years before the attenuation of faculties
bestowed the gift of attrition the contrite
cowed the crows in the nation's field

where all slumber enumerates the transient
all particular variables cannot consist
nor their insistence conclude the foregone
insinuations of the deeply permitted

deviance the norm of essentials
in vines of veritas whose numbers
enervate the season of its living
the persistent emulate their decrees

a reason freezing the fortitude
of logistics pensioning numerical
storms for the very bidding forms
a consensus of disinformed intent

numbers content on sensations of self-
referentiality forgiving the numbness
of transgression's wit amid the recycled
retainers of attorneys overpowered

litigious slumbers snore transient jokers
before motifs breed their muted indigence
muffled against the shuffling old
and their hordes of leathered pigeons

the malcontents climb the store
inventory breeds itself with conjure
disdaining the bold the stuffy
pertaining to dissidents of stations

unserviced amid the horded influx
of trampolines insurgent in their springs
resurgent in their urgent modalities
scuffling against the pain of weather

and parallels marching down
the sentries of time's centurions
guarded in their geometric mists
amid songs of seedy fortitude

## Ancient Secrets

Indigo laughter withers the sphincter petals
under the hyacinthine moors. The bloodletting
ensues,

bright with chicory's plunge across the jerkwater estuary,
a statue white with providence, its yield tumescent. Pasts
of futures unforetold await hieroglyphic ruins riddled with
sphinxes.

Hyenas peddle their tragic girth
amid chimerical manors, borne
on weightless flurries

or the moment
of its whim.

In hateful fury indigent peddlers speak
moons of flowered begetting. There, let-me-nots
abuse

light's explicable lunge against a staring lurk,
incandescent in its omniscient flow. Beneath its
cast sutures stem the obsidian ivory's glowing bone.
Withholding sundials begets desire among coded
fields.

The myrrh of inkblot offerings
roar shock at the least unwieldy
perceptions scurrying

heavily to weight its
hymn to momentum's

dromedary feast. The water rises, the flood
planes its red bevel. The devilish humor of deserts
prevails

dry with the lure of rain. Its glare stems
the bud that nips its barren heels, trips its
fast future over a slow sundial, meridian with
haste.

Plotting stock exchanges
diatonically, the greedy correct
blossoms with

sediment & omens
that stem its climb

beyond the melodies of the sun. Forgetting
its own mystery, the secret reveals itself to historic
rubicons

unlettered with decay. Its pure strain
seals the depth of runic privilege, locking
alien vertebrae in time capsule chambers
arid

& spotted with red moss
dried brown. Its blood steeps
sentiment at its

bottom where myth &
time seal all momentum.

## Apocalypse Later

photosynthetic Sufis whirl neon umbilicals
barbarian cries stare down triangles value face
crypto-voltaic messengers crown the one
true breathing through motor ellipses

and prophets shall fare their brushes

motorcades stream spinning leather
sycophants emerge granting full authority
to purging measures of dispute irresolute
and unrequited

there the hair shall assail

womblike predicates
acerbic natal union suits
first national then fine asked
effervescent shops to stop

the flow

of nutrients

over

purple protocols impassioned
with tincture where grooms distinctly
bridle instinctive tuxedo showers that hide

the secrets of Rue Nee

## As Moving Sound Thinks

Somnambulatory vouchers past due
seal your floor praise your stealing
excessive days mount candles like mares.

Stay.

Inches flinch contiguous
ambiguities defiant riot fluidities
hot wax eels lock doors open.

Praise thumbs.

Mumble certainties stumble
space erases mores the vacuum abhors
with triplicate replication of

dextrous leaps gone digital

## Balancing Axe

Metastatic cattle pry their prodding wedge.
It multiplies their plodding battle, dries the
flurrying cells cursing the edge of orange
with teeth benighted. Alluring folds tell covens
of furies, animistic with primal grief. Cold
ovens bake mornings fresh with liquid sun.
Taste relief in the form of prattle. Baste
eclectic belief systems with carcinoma's
ecstatic flay. Cinema verite's simplistic
lens folds the coptic nerve against retro-
spective foresight. An old swerve upends
the mantis praying brief pistons dance
against the wind. Rescind the suture.

Of its own kind there can be no other. Without regard for the high-
est the mist shall dangle past rewards in the space of the other.
Facing the wind's back braces no returns. Nor the taxonomy of ruin.
Spacious in its lamented fist breeds ospreys. For the difference of
autonomy no dependents yield. The perspicacious tax unseals its
musty womb, revealing musty tunes of splendid rancor. Intuit uncom-
mon mummies tracing leathered flesh in the music of band aids. Or
the unkind angle shall deny among the last throes its humid lover.

In the static battle cry the trodding pledge.
It panoply scares rotting cattle, belies the
hurrying swell cursing the alleged storage
of beliefs uncited. Telluric folds swell love
in buried antihistamines with timed belief.
Old lovers ache boring flesh, quit the one
haste unleashing the storm of battle. Taste
electric briefs, their pistons stiff aromas on
a plastic tray. When enema verifies implicit
blends hold synaptic verve against hetero-
sexuals cold, upright as old nerves intend
the antics betraying grief. Sisters, stance
defends their kin, the sins of lurid future.

## Call and Response Under Crystal Lake

*for the Middletown Creative Orchestra*

ambient crystal shakes the floor's
electrostatic convulsion of chickens
roosting home the tenor lays
where groundwork

says the sly eagle

safe in the nuance of ecstasy its subtle intent emerges
a classic cacophony caffeined to its first utterance
mindsurge omen momentous becomes kind urge
entranced with the nape of jurassic kittens

their incessant declarations

tin-pan tympanis synth with cumulus accretions
accrue syntactic betrayals sympathetic to time
and monied nations immolating their successes
no madder than short the time

its call to dissuade

the others obscure its truth with nurtures
of motherly pensions procuring fruited loons
in traces of accident the doctors seed
beyond lectures of intensity

protests of plurality

conjunctions engage the sweated ones
pythons of their own configuration or stature
while melodies linger in stations
the music of

clinch the unabetted

## Circling Bushnell Park

The foregone occlusions that ossify traffic
include barter as a means of crossing the arterial
hem, its stationery target a pencil for alms. The poor,
palms outstretched as their suffering rows,
emote sanctity and exhaust.

The patience of mufflers in winter,
open doors to lean, transported protrusions of sclerotic nuance
against infusions of statutory denial

wherever popcorn sheds
its name, decries the military rank of gasoline. Towed fumes
tame their octane with virile aspersions of natural gas

breeding sameness among all the nameless that apply
their visceral truths to virtual emblems, silencing the somber music
of cyber-punks wearing air guitars and shoulderstraps
under the hood of the

oil-burning discourse of lamplights
frozen to honorariums on horses in traffic circles staring madly
at passers buying unsightly memorabilia:

aquariums without fins,
purchase untamed by Everest, unnamed winds in the slurred
face of coherence dribbling its winter chin across capsules

of unsightly gelatin brandishing its purpose
for the statements of the unwielding plurality. Chromosomes
chant mercurial blather pent with flurry. Wishing
for fish and pentium futures

bid sundials on the wave
of the concourse. Frayed trials stray on course. Off the
projected savings a bitter trajectory

breeds denial
in the airspace of the afflicted. Handwritten tomes declare
the moribund more abundant in their preservation

of the vacancies

that only the cross-town

traffic can utter

## Circling the Horizon

Coruscating the dentally premature
gives tooth to acts of generic dissidence
fluent in their distant entirety. In places where
the squeamish scream their druidic intent
the dissonance of invention flourishes:

less begun by the fathers the prairie seekers
want horizons in their midst /

a circling of wagons
trained toward the future's

circular ledge.

Where Hell in its meatless preambles
drives mothballs to sample furs the cloth falls
over naked pistons of the damned. Not even
novocaine can help their turgid pleas, their
contrite theories of prudent restoration; despite

the sheer force of it its ambiguity. The preambles
dismiss the naked pledge as.

Hortatory galvanization
musters all in the call of its dreadful sweep

of pillars

## Country Life at Sea

1.

rural backroad benign
the plural manifests its leaves
trenchant smoke detectors climb
in the distance

the vessels steam lumber in midriffs
autumnal harvest reaps its roosters
claim delays to sustenance approved

softness humbling itself
to deities bereft of culted rumors
in relaying the aboriginal truth
to multiple vectors

where insects conjugate satin verbs
dens howl their cabalistic majesty
coven bakes root in pinetar sex

2.

where opposites retract
prehensile tethers amidst their tragic glow
its branches shift  more abundant
pleasures of infant jest

inside the chests of barreled sailors
insurgent shore leaves displeasured
roadsides in the wake of the unspoken

amnesty attractive bargains to be sure of
when no uncertainties know bounds
or leaps to faith in cattle measured heaps
dwindling with stargaze

the mighty weeps astounding crossed prairies of day
light in the sky pounding rare electrodes of transients

foreign to the gluttonous heaps of wool & mollycoddle

3.

the sweep of praying mantises weeps its enchantment
the influx of essence deflorescent is its weighty sleep
whose existence replays the antic tonnage
across apothecary fields of rustic intent
where the indentured pray for treatment

in suites of fullness
imbued with clippers
autonomous sledge
of cruelties bestowing

the tribune's edge
rips open its gravel sea
towing foremost streets
casualties behind them

where quarries of the damned
oscillate their fibrous tissue
ants sing the yeast of algae

**Demolition Fedora**

Transpire the lucubrating offset.
The curmudgeons undertow their
lugubrious lament. Instantaneous
the flow of rivers

and content expressing
its cement bulge in the navelry of orange.

Without its purview
the scope of dopamine cannot
discharge its aura, nor stir in it
horrible contempt for the turn-

styled. Masses
spur its awful genus. To the stylus

of fair played in its
moribund vinyl stack, whose very blackening

asserts the tribe's
striation as a statement of a sovereign nation

eating the heads
of its guillotine dismembered in honor of the

Nor the equity
its horses unchained where nectar plumb

leads its scary seed
to breed in the moist crevice of the inanimate

chosen by the masters of decree
in postulate entry, oozing pus in
trees barren of paper. The rape
was well accounted for,

the papers said
behind the fonts of readers

dreading the hope
of the many for they threw, their
sentries run the pencil of orgasm,
thin as slumber, naked as deluge,

or its messianic tint
invidious in its dapple sway & ointment.

For the conjoined translucents
panicking with flutes, loins & goat hooves

to bare their momentous downroll
up hills where they top prophecy with acorns, declare

the militance of furriers
abjurious to the naked forerunners

in their sharkened tint. The night
before the ostentation stark in its
rude appeal turns sanguine at
the sun, instant

bides its time
as distance of the cowering gray.

Where the hovels
snatch the blue teeth of night to scratch
at crucial sediments, ignite raw density.
Intent in its sentiment: who to demolish

the catwalks of the towering shovel

**Eulolooming**

languid epistolary nuanced l'amour
seeded beside the jerkwater sill
betrays need with vertiginous wants

daunting in its pallor
the subtle disorientation
fugues its haunting memories

distilling the vapor of pastel

pentacular in its gravidity
memory its multiple birth

impaled on the pit of memory
its thoughtful pith instilled

through traces of wanton magic

her lesson delayed its quickening lesion for the participle of its lingering frenzy all tips anointed with the tragic of sway foretold in forests of ancient enchantment secrets calling gold a misled alchemy weighted with her forbidden name falling cold upon death's ears weaving the worldly sabbaths of weir as the words of the wary foretold

breath quickening behind the thicket
of sensory diminuendo its innuendo

common knowledge among the certified
density of begotten lore

the raven's approach
delayed the bloodletting dialogue

of healing leeches soporific
getting under kin

increasingly alabaster

Poe's prophesy

of fragrant skin

turned old

## Fetch a Calling Star

a gaseous transience has befallen
the ascetic platitudes rent from
audacity's multi-faceted scream

intransigent in the amorous flow
the latitudes course the teeming wedge
of mendacity's aesthetic

horses stream the river's crossing
while the hedge traces its placid fortitude
across remuneration's bathetic sea

where compensatory overtures
masticate the many from the chew
and the courses deliberate

their fumes laboriously intent
upon pathetic displays of entry
where forces recourse their doom

and switches rush the Moses bull
masticating with matador's lambent
dosage climbing the seaward

star gazing at the plummet
rent from the face of the sundry sky
its resources well deployed

each surface razing flames
from the sameness meant to cloy
the ploys from the steaming ledge

## Fire and Water

Filamental fire needles evergreen
eats the millstone cannery
tossing albatrosses causing
photsynthesis among aluminum follicles
of mass hysteria. Where wisteria tombs
the Mongols horde rooms of purple. Hazes
amaze the protons of their watchful
neutrality. Plurality beckons reckoning
purity, its allure fleeting sail oats.
Doting on the albacore of happenstance
the neutron eats inertia, heats
triangular rescue missions.
Tissues erupt with wine tentacles
mentally imbued, a stew of pixels
grown ticklish in the light. The sticklers
sight demands cancellation. Its laughter
peels layers of night off leather metals.
Elemental desire hardens the void
where annoyance trains supreme tracking
backs of reverse to myriad pilgrims.
Diverse reckonings beckon allure annoyed
hoarding purple, they graze. Cattle and sheep
sleep in the pit of nectarine diplomacy,
their cordless umbilicals mumbling
pecuniary concerns. The liniment turns
the quest on a maze: where from go, we here.

## Going Hollywood at Home

The stench of pedicure & fingernail polish
collages fetishes & mother's wishes
to whom the dreary need apply
scarlet legends of terra cotta in winter.

Hinterland starlets expire in terra cognita,
wrenched from edifice to attrition. Wearily
they try the justice arbitrarily scaling their skin
with instruments of skintight percussion.

The non-arrivals exude preclusion
as a means of identification, oven-baked
buck naked exhibitions on morning talk shows
tearing at the blank screen's crevasse.

Moreso the fusion of silent musics
withholding consent & taxing intent
of spurious fashion. The attraction takes
hold of cold water's first hot flashes,

their bold leaps notwithstanding
the empty auditorium, the leeches
of glory emanating persuasive dim
innuendoes that pass for wit. Forward

the words march, meaning themselves
into neon others dreaming passion's
steam from vessels emptied of voice,
their noise glowing coldly in the dark.

## Heavy Mettle

pyrite portmanteau
ghouls fold glimmers
swim to bottom's surface
among the surfeit lies

true to formlessness
despite ultimatum's criteria
for trying rhapsodies

dyes pupae of purple
sweaters aluminum crinkles
winks its scaffold eye
at butterflies cocooning

thistle embryos
so goes the process
recessive in its thinking

## Hoarse Latitudes

particles emotive lost to saws
betray the cause of sassafras
the jaws yield to their peculiar

currency among lost minds
articles promote dead fields
strewn with cost overruns

all projections its trajectory
in sight offers new particles
array the ruinous motive

toss the crawfish a tide
the night directions bred
horses proffer demoted

blades detonated aside
injections offer the most
profligate days ahead

of tight reins accosted
inflections draw the wish
of hush-filled coffers

## Home Entertainment

Artfully the breathing
stops armchairs in their stream
a delight

only the wicked can
esteem.

Interiors do not gossip tapestries

where furniture abounds.

Central

to the integer

of place lies geometry as bed of concrete
muscled to shore, then inland, a sequence
of no germane order to the lawn in its
personal configuration,

though the polyester servants
master the inanimate in delusory
fashions of control, the which breathe

numeric necessities

as summaries of a season forever remembered
by doilies in their pain.

Wherever the couches end
the plunge must remain severe & the arm ledge
a terror to a still-laced domain

where furniture impounds

the polyester masters
so numerous, in their fashion
every delusory breath

a necessary integer

at

center

## Homeward Winds

smithies awash the candlestick's snore
intrusive the more unwashed it gets elusive
beset aside the full moon tide begets striding

manly indifference chugs its tugboat pipe
going down for the yardage first its throws
frame inference astride the lugs of brown

reclusive substance the integers of chance
eat its crown grow exponents intentionally
sweeping the rug under its fractious number

of udders cannot refill the utmost tank
dillying anvils across the sea so dizzily
spewing angoras of Catskill radiance

redundant with canine effortless its tail
of abundance draining the sail fool blown
in his own wind seeking reprobation

its homegrown subsidiaries despair
the fluvial stadium of cost control
lost to the current of air unknown

**In Process**

prevaricate
stretch limos in triplicate nylons
the purple undoing

heroic aerobics shun
the untamed one etches intricate
pilings renew

ingots stamped margins
their largess ensuing vipers
variant of doing

form stretches
intimate wheels in flux
four arid etchings

set almost
to mewing of crystalline molasses
stretches true

sticklers along
misconstrued pundits of the blue-blood
masses heap

carob blessings
turning form into contest reviewed
harum-scarum

diplomats declaring
cloisters of nunneries in snake's nests
free of all

shame blaming
those in process to baring the naked monologue
under review

**In Pursuit**

Gentle danger
hawk the sky
stalk leaves
trail behind

walk deliberate
futons trembling
dissemble feet

save distance
interest accrues
while you face
water      Stall

flight's stumbling
neutrons collect
electric nuance

free the fleeting
stew renew the seed's
faintly rumble

## In the Places of Nature

swan down where
neo-con bulbs hold their sway
inordinate
their staying power

triplicates diverse
as influence bestowed where
nuances
unfold fraying tendrils

there but for
the grace of playing fawns
coordinates
meet their vectors

insurgent their dance
primitive praying rites delayed
autumnal
stayed to cower

defacing the visage
betraying the vengeance of rain
duplicitous
powers distant traces

**Issues of Theme**

banshee wails trumpet
the weevil's evil synchronicity
with Hamlet's revenge

its field of non-sensory picking
vibrates against fields of rudder
wooden in their alacrity

plots
as the wheel of color
turns

purple with midnight nectar
ocarinas divulge the fence howls of cats

lost oils emerge
knots channeled through the dyes
enclothing indigo night

its lavender of black
safe in the sudden pluck of sky
from cloud on down

nimble fingers
snatch color, snatch soul
from the berries of gin

## Moon Tide

Empty the wind
seeds. The down below
solicits all blue tidings

wherein those derided call their know / its sequence
deny the factor of implicit shame. Its victory seeding

illicit temptation
to and fro elicits the ball
bounce / added to the yard

indicate of same yet never in its stead.

Force, its true equivalent,
blindly leads its swaggered might
blithe to the spirit's wiggling

toe, disregards
its stately purpose.
As declared

among the rhetoric of the dead

the harrow must try
all vividness aside
to wheel its spectral tray

to the south. The locus demands spraying, irately
proposing its truisms aside, where neatly the transposed

follow
the warming trends allowed out of season
-s allayed

by the shortage of prophecy.

Allow the cyclical sequence its
beginning, its myth of continuity disposed
on the reefs of shallow waters

corals snake. Its purpose
hoarded among natives
in their foreign lands

seeks neither fortitude                    nor certainty in the allowance

of forbearing
horse rides concurrent with the dappling
moon mares

holding captive the midnight sky

**On Alienation**

the occlusion of dawn's sediment
transports the weary wind to a diaspora unknown
to those of its own kind

foreign to the other's touch
alien to the sense of weather

akin to igneous recluses
the abstruse cabal elicits the fall
of donors grown on soil

filtered through photosynthetic modalities
prototypes for oaths against the sun

& its rising  spears
cumulonimbus loincloths
the warrior's shield

blue colors the terror within

## One Steppe at a Time

1.

over the flow the ottoman wails
the injustice of armchair cossacks

steppes across the plane

of knowing

the juncture shredded below
the hassocks of the threadbare
dare to tread

their ingrained depth

showing righteous dread

of hubcaps in the hardwood fist
of right-wristed rumors left to the sinister
instead of the mightily before them

or behind

the closet shelves its declarations of interest
in favor of intestate principal

bestowing amazing lace

on the doilies of the disenchanted

2.

the automanics below disdain
the Siberian trolley's arctic flowering

their towering vessels over-slung

with ancient curricula

disjunctures breed octuplets of discontent
meant strictly as dodecaphonic polyphony
angling cassocks against

the orthodox waging

aging in their distance

way before the wooden frontage
stakes draculian effect for the right
to deface its naked claim against

the front

of hickory reparations tailored
to dickering principle

remiss in its dutiful transience

past the brooding merchants chanting

3.

dolor has its concrete center here
fiscal in its duodecimal splendor of austerity

gaping chairs in equatorial tundra in the wake of nomads

spouting sheep the cold sleep rumors
its free delivery to the isolation
of victims

lurid in their tenacity's

fervid garden

where hardened hucksters soil
the primrose lava with ambidextrous
duties appointed

with caribou feathers

protection against the birdseed
of inclement forecast

weathered against

the mammoths breaking moody through their thaw

## Opposing Seats at the Old Cedar

The young mark fresh from dream
chants current fashion against tired poets

opposes
the weary modernistic yoke:
elementary stanza

rhythm
verse
rhyme.

Late poets, worn out
from middle school distinction, reflect
against the new-fashioned young:

high
school
stress.

Modern young adults
in college throb new-sprung animal seminary:

poets against pulsation.

Neoteric form
peculiar to poets
versus cadence:

additional call,
fresh vibration...

holler about
opposing tattoos.

The current mantra:
modernistic carols, minstrels
against measure's supplementary sing.

The bandwagon starts at muse.
Further numbers fasten persuasion,
beginning with troubadour

fronting tempo

extra couplet characteristic

of possession's poignant pulse.

The original harness,
an inclination peculiar to authors,
passionately stresses
disparate buckle marks outside of cogitation.

Notwithstanding accentuation,
the unseasoned hayseed's appearance
starts at dream, withstands the bluster

of a dissimilar young character

peculiar to street singers:

the Anterior Sentinel

**Palabras**

palaver forever
the end of widows peaking
across endless amplitudes
longitudinal in their sympathetic
displays a way, from windows
eking out gritty triplicates.
In feathered drawers filled
with boas

constrict the lessons
of lesions unlearned
paper. Scraping squeaks
its metallic tint
leaking over generic
bubbles.

                    Or, as
the colloquia say:
idiomatic staying power
sways hulas in the wheeze
of wedlock's oars. Deep
as the dread keeps, solarity
unlocks replete squalls
in restaurants of the thinking:

                    a cunning

                         of brutal specificity

## Prophecies of Matters Past

Leaner transplants accrue
the immortal dust, its foliage meaner
than lances.

That boil the artifact of presence
ensues, a participle in the. Losing
its essence to graying pontificators

the oracle spreads
the instance of its meaning
to other.

Incidents into intent
of vice into versus
the animal plots its

flow pagewise, desiccating arrows
flush with context, devoid of cement.
The necessary intrusions belie

underneath its salted web
mere tonnage. Mortified mummies gasp
their infants

grasp maternal rage, eternal
verities stricken with oxide plumes.
A fuming dissonance depletes

its range.
Smothers its berth with carriages
of Miss Demeanor

and her mannered few,
the vagaries of insouciance
abetted by razor clams.

Nor can the empty assuage their relief
among those stricken with intent
(the form that follows its looming

apodictic. Along the sainted path
to scented apocrypha the fumes of lost incentive
gain. Words to describe their histories

forward in the name of trajectory
assaulted suede. Those delayed
responded with fits of glossolalia

incorporated
into charters of the vast.
Undertaking

coffins as effort,
the fluent respond
with life or death

tangents. Their plangent plumes
feather the gloom in their midst
with olives twisted to dickens

charmed with feats unfold-
ed in the innards of the dead
merchants of venison

rife with miscellaneous allusion
a protrusion into the foregone
mysteries

of

conclusion

**Rocky Ground**

The liquid outbursts
of the unconfronted igneous
affront public sediment

layered its obsequious
strands arrest the seat of disquiet
amid lava's ubiquitous flow

belying its turbid intent
to ossify the slow sentiment
still flowing inside

bestowing juncture
on rafts of petrified fossils
seeking a phylum

from the octagonal mist
rocking ashen feats of closure
across the orange sky

**Route 44 West**

The Cantonese of Avon
bark inscrutably white.
Bagels hamper steadfast
guardrails. Trains ensue
trans(limits of)gression,
expression's black skin
in Latin. Pigs, all of them.
Claim the stop. Pop the
summer's picnics. Illicit
sexless Stepford Wives
await dairy farms explicit
in their ambivalence.
Exquisite in their
equivalence the rains bare
the burden of crossing.

## Sargasso in C

fiscal endorphins leap
the luminary's gradient
enamored

of cockle's muscles

in the dark

the savage flies unbrowned
in its incessant grilling its steam
purported for the mammals
of the Western Ledge

no purpose unfilled
proposes roses in hunches
uncloseted

delight roars its clamor

in protest

water ripples & churns
its idle waves a dream recumbent
on bellies of sawgrass
turning tidal at the tangent

guiding the path
outside itself the ruins of Atlantis
pivot on the mollusk

memory conceals the opus

in the mist

the waters feel calcified pain
draining its ambitious personifications
on the moss of camels abetting
the primal need for stasis

wild things grow
acclaimed in the longitudinal
myth deriding

amplified silence underscores

its dragnet of fish

## Sunday Ware

frayed cuffs chalk the cote melange
its nether spice weathered in the lain
niceties of sea tracks the stalkers heft
under moons bereft of walk rough
legends of cursive pageantry

the glitter bestows its presence
seeds the encumbered frown
betrayed to the fixity of its own
vexation

the vain where admirals bare their tread

slate becomes its shadowed presence
walks the girth of waists unbound
by tremors in the earthen night
nor sound of cloven birth

enough to spread its gaunt-
let treasure found the galleon
haunted among the fossils
of fluorescence

detailing
the travesty that derails its majesty

through ciphers of tragic wants

there the pain of initiative waits
to punish the travails of nomads
dead inn there

wake the subtleties of tirade
instead

unfailing

in its endless dread of narrative

bed or breakfast in its nuisance

or flow beyond the
needs rippling the water
with terse in chased

error its hot pursuit

the chair beguiles the tragic

its nuance unrequited

the gray suit of terror

once again meets with the hunger hurried

to best

another airy station in position
the diatribe of hunger ensues the plaintiff
measured in reactive bounds untethered stinting
emotion flourishes under shaded plots of basil nourishes
the trickery of the unencumbered seed laid to rest at the latest ruin

no sequence more for any torn
dry goods elaborate the frame
incipient fluidity proffers

netting another with its cache
afraid to walk the coat or flange
needy foot pedals of their music

remote the challenge of its offing

silent in umbral magic its timbral tragic hue

the tufts that greet him under strange gray

## Techno Wash

loquacious lint
balls dry automatic cotton
technocrats ensure

ribald hosts forgotten
chances clench the unsure
cinch with calls

of pure impact
debasing  wet silk tracing
its satin string

alluring voice
springing the lurid dance
of triplicate matter

into the turgid grasp
of strangled metamorphoses
turbid in their demented

technologies of the weary
forgotten in the languor of opium
dons the bleary spring

rains falling over raw
tufts of data metempsychosing
inside the dryer's spin

## Thanksgiving with Frankie Laine

Is tan bull
in constant
in opal

turkey lurks

if con stanton
no pal then its
tambour

gets the works

instant pull
of constant ennoble
then ids

stand full
of constantine
opiates

stem pull
of cons standing
noble

turkey quirks

## The Archaeology of the Present

1.

Stark raving sane
the words inflame the vestibule.

Fools of inner light
curse the autumn wind and rain

remain lucid through
all crimes as rescinded as portals

to those craving
the wisdom of purple madness.

2.

The flies disincline the tertiary of substance,
a remonstrance not soon forgotten. Its chastening
revokes the pledge

of foregone eras
saving green stamps of post-mortem passage.

To assuage the threat of
unseamly demeanor cloth sews its vesicle shut-

down at the plant. The crisis
of herbal necessity grows
tales of naked haberdashery

in hunters of primordial lassitude.
Verbal precocity rises, its stance
a thoughtful grow among the neon

ferns. Days glow and ties die,
the climate insubstantiates the inveterate
of their clothing

a strip mauling
its discounted patrons in the terminal.

3.

Collages juxtapose

the archaeology of the present

ruin

its nascent trajectory spacing time.

Ruin

embraces what colleges oppose:

the fossils grew in the caustic night

portends

acidic their constituencies a gloom

portends

visions of arid tautology in its arc

juxtaposes collage

port ends ruin

4.

The metaphysics of duct tape

denote the unassailability

of fluidity's flossed virtue.

Where, with all, not with standing
its per, mutations deride the flux
alone. The stone, when seated
fails to rise promptly at beckon's call.

The fall of electricians from grace

braces its availability

on triggers haired from horses lost

5.

Sequence bestows the measured call
with trade-offs from jackknife fecundity.
The errant nights moon the sun. In this
respect their nuance unfolds crystal

waters unfurled their flagging vapors
ingesting pedicures free of acrimonial
substance. One foot washes an other.
Disclosures of unity reveal separate

lotions. The treasured fall will grow
jaded within its jarring dissonance,
or magic will raid tragic maypoles,
diminishing their faded sustenance

as trinkets wrinkle and sag. Distance
patrols the intimate. The inanimate toss
their bulge. Raided animus profligate
indulges its pre-carcinogenic disarray.

6.

Sharks pave inane
frames of bloody ventricles with saw teeth.

Collages tame fools
whose juxtaposing tentacles deny their claim.

Tracing lines shape
visions of the blind with tinted glasses.

Staving pain saves
portaled masses from the weight of decision.

**The Downs of Feathered Joy**

dance their scapular shells
tidy with uncombed nails and nutrients
saturated marble fat heaps its globes

tethers nails concurrent shut
rope at the nether ends of coral
sputter through oral storms of hiss

dismissed schools of darkness
huddle amid weathered tentacles
skeptics breed their ruination

selves of others swell humble
diversions of inverted pride
divergent on all contractual terms

of endearment while cannibals
feed on vegetable omelets no egg
remains intact in its intractable

essence which came first
shall also come last as hinges
ductile on the circumspect

aboriginal muster of the opiate
indeeding tactile approvals of the
circus spectral in its aim

## The Hard-Shell Approach

the carapace of fruition
knows the seed of wanting
its gauntlet run to nylon

ampersand molecules spit neon
convergent amber in the dusk
smug in its tawdry thrill

stocking oscillations
the bunkers declare their visibility
orchid on the half-shell

stealing their hard-sell hunkers
the casualties of ossified bawds
instill the favor of centipedes

husking free the vapors of trust
they exceed no unknown bounds
to leap their expert lineage

or tall buildings with single
crustaceans lounging by the pool
or stream of thought

tinkered with a dam
of crescents rendered obsolete
by moons under pistachio

## The Landlocked at Sea

The igneous trigger of lava floes
fizzles the sloe gin with its number.
Inconsequential frigates boom and sizzle,
glow. Descends the night.

Pits of darkness overall heed slumber
its depth of ruin healing standard tunes
of their metrical splitting. A midriff

of continental stasis appends the setting
to weddings of gaseous fusion

elemental in the candid secret
of pineal flux. The row progresses slowly

to rumble static pavements of yellowed brick.
The foresight of tomatoes continues unabated,
the magic of its tricks snickers.

Gratuitous threats.
Discharge the tumble seating there.

Engorge the spirit dismal in its flux,
in the suction of prism light:

the consequence of numbered schisms
exulting in the netting gain no prophet sees

but grossly. After its taxing dividends
the fortunate squander their jigger of rocks.
In their quivers the bows denote: tension
grows. Slow delight:

ensembles of digital fortitude caress
the wilderness of discount pottery

and clams:

the hard sell of their half-shell approach,
the trickery of the open face

spams networks of indecision
with forks stalking the multitudes
talking in tongues

with their mouths full. The crudity of oil
slippery in its deceit

fouls the quandary
of lewd butchers sweating in the shoreline

jungle of furs. Tripping over sedimentary masts
of centuries past their lapidary futures cannot hold
the tortures of the insane. The will stirs triggers
in the sharks above the cistern chapel.

Where Atlantis seeds its holy fluid
the desert awaits its stark menu.

**The Last Word**

admirable frictions peruse
the truth endlessly seeking interdiction

a sequence of what was that ensues

present grows tense
in the grammar of physiognomy

its lexicon demure
&
passive

in confrontation with
weakening desperate equivalents

sense denies its other

trial seeks its own
jury among the self-serving summons

of judges

engaged in massive
deliberations of accidental

trysts enticing laundromats

voyeurs dicing squid
on tables at the backs of railroad cars

the clack begets its sow

amid the franchise
the disenfranchised grow antic

with semantic concerns

the frantic darts of
ignominy dominate the frenzy

of the unmeaning

**The Mollusk Follicle**

Crying bells await the caller
who hurries his name in dandruff
waking. Field of orange smut
away from mollusk invention
intent on its propensity, starting,
senses a bird bent on its pray
this autumn day where fairs linger
and turnstiles gray.

In the silence of the loudmouth
only the dollop can complain.

Shells abound hating balls
found wallowing. In distant hairs
of field each waking to steam
the misanthrope's wet intention
of dream, to be misread like texts
of the druid telegraph. The punch
dines on fast faces lasting beyond
the call, all this for the sake.

In the dolor of dreams
surely a mountain must contain

burdens. Tether most weathering
get here to place instead the leather
of thought's first buckle.
Insistent on the truth of liniment
cosmically aligned as through each
and each signs reach inclines
to knuckle. Under water dreaming
the sun's first beam of hair atones for
staring at its porcelain root

where the slalom of screams
devours its heart with a plantain

## The Ova of Blue Necessity

Imbroglio the chicken hatches
broil the surmising slug coiling its lugubrious intent
cementing the truisms of fiction
where hatchers dare

their spurious spawn.

Beware the sagacious,
their treasures mute. Their pleasures,
invidious as they seem,
denote the enmity of tangents

in fury drawn, or content.

Their sentiment broods at junctures of the bowel
precipitate in their waste. In their case, to reciprocate
the enemies, transients accrue.

Statements of purple dread,
chaste as nicotine berated, for its salmon glow
the ashes below. The tundra multiply

slow as ice in rapid transit:
the glacial epoxy. Dilapidated
wan tons stew, grow nicely

where chamber pots summon
the humbled among us. There they flow
their thickening brew to

whomever their intent.

A secret yield: the glottis
shields its myriad silence with unwieldy
truisms. Jihads for the ambient

schisms wield delirious

prawns protesting

the intransigent fury of cement, its trenchant discontent
a matter fixed in form of passing comment. The latter
an unlikely place to climb

over matters under review,
the ova of blue necessity's neon blink
erasing the trace of ruined embryonics.

In muting their anticipation
the farragoes of beaten retreat
seek solace in the libraries

of the dead. Their harrowing
farrow of dread intangibles stares, intent
with coils of transmitting

data unremitting

in its propensity for jugular
containers drawing blood of regents unborn,
an immensity committed against
the fertile eggs

quietly emitting

intangible futures

to their distrust

## The Poets on Super Bowl Sunday

Invidious
the tentacles of fallacy chatting in the vestibule

exhibiting pinkies upthrust with purple disregard.
Myth discards the oval trenchant with hammers.
What matters with cards is the slope of mirrors,

the stammer notwithstanding its crux,
assiduous

in the rain the chard swims, vegetable hope
canards its ruin. Yet wrenches demand fixity,
aplomb the rune of our ledge, a tomb dies

rigorous
in the wake of prohibiting deities

vigorous in their flux. The next successor
vibrant with the seed of amoebic discourse
disguises resourcefulness with clamor

insidious as the steak choking the smoke alarm.

## The Political Is the Personal

Fried Chernobyl chicken soup
tears alchemy behind the eyes. Automobiles
beget the gratuitous attacks of mirrors
projecting fearful reflections of three-mile interiors.

Wastelands of words and wantnot
snowshoe tracks wheel across the treaded steppes
of tie-dyed years to attack the myriad foregoners

weeping their invasion. In the mist
coastal waterways demand transfusions
of sand. Their atmospheric midst sheds

no daylight.

The gray sun laughs my last illusion
past confusion returns the present

The tundra soup of the turgid soul
melts fingers, melts minds, melts Reubens
by the hand, smelts iron ore sanity.
Interior acid brightens autumnal folly
leaves fall ashen, perennial arctic shade
over the shredded vanity of Pittsburgh.

When calamity hits
land war mines one's Russian ego
begins its baking powder
calumny a recipe

for government shortages.

Encouraging fossils need apply.
Reckless danger meant sending winds to caution
the petrification process of faulty perimeters:

radio activist alarm clocks march
intently off borders of Dali paintings.

Flat Earth theory drips the interior's cutting edge.

The gray sun laughs its fast allusion
vast intrusions prefer the lessened.

The Reuben in Russian winter
eats no other land war but Rimbaud's
derangement of the sentence

a snowless desert legion in their midst
seeks intensity to conquer the missing vacant
who raid the last night's glow of the dark
retro-Pop artists boast neon aurora borealism

into the mirror raping faces that grow on the ark.

The hibernating soul of
nuclear winter protests thalidomide obtrusion.
Confusion rains acrid steams

& Siberian kings
husky in their peasant state
three miles from mind's grip

let islands slip through forked trellises of fingers.
Deserts of water begetting the future protest in seclusion.

If reason laughs half-mast diffusion
its last protrusion returns the unsent

**The Sacrificial Lam**

wanted posters want
nothing over exposure
to blue clerks

nor its trajectory
seeking missile-to-heat surfaces
whatever depths may reveal

unwanted toasters post
frayed warnings in black trouser cuffs
against boxing ears

wary their varied pursuits
pinstriped with largess and vermicelli
as they always do

who should haunt
mirrorless reflections dissecting
the other's elf

holiday vampires
ambient as spiral scare chases
mad hatters of blood

## The Syntax of Futures Tense

Choruses of lateral cries Suez
accordingly. The disposition rises
batter a broken record tracing
vinyl histories redux. The influx
of surgical memories posits
defloresence among its

mysteries of humors to chance a position erasing
tumors defacing histories of rumored surgical staples
of life among

Elephantine mollusks ordain
the postulates of the mummified
few. If any. The moreso retracts

didactically the flatter of the two,
humors the subcutaneous intent inherent in the unwilling
whose test their fingers

To disdain the limits of lingering content
adrift in empty vesicles seminal in their
drain. A fluidity that masks the task of the

Process itself begets the many of the few
so large in number as to prevent the continuity of discord
and its related

Harmonies clash. The trash of sound
smashing  particles adrift in the sea
of meaning, the rift uplifting the leaning

tide shifts. Inside the salt swell
a Morton's umbrella continues
to smell detergent muffles ruffling

the torrid green, its turgid flow
boring the earth's core

to bovine slumber it goes, kneading modules of infinite plastic
elated with elastic that chews the very fat plating its nodules.
Recording its

rash of innocence through dissonance
the assonance passes its mustard to myths
of near meaning. The word invents.

Its spleen. Paces its venom
with a cobra's neck among the coral
snakes abound across a/the

lawn tennis courts. The mission aborts.
The captain tugs his boat. Attrition cuts
short tradition. Long before the after

## The Third Ultimatum

Interlocutory degrees heat rooms made for sweeping
meat's revenge from the obfuscation of clarity.
Only the needless unfortunate show charity known
for its leeway and panty-hose. To free the rampant
of highways rage stages roads replete with coaches
and wells pennies wish for Fargo at bottom sand.
It's a dollar hill to climb on, solid footing
of summer ice---a trap perhaps to those above
the butchery. Its legion speaks to all concerned
such as the remnants of the silo hills much adored
by the frenzied wrenches entrenched in sidelong tombs
of terminal hassle germinate speed rings cylinders
pistons whistle protons thistle electrons eat the
very heart of plumbing fixtures, gestures of vanity

while rotors rite the roots of dismay affirmed
contumely praises obsolescence in its own name
never to be repeated. Its retreat an advance
on the chance treated as mettle scores settle
stores advance consuming propaganda cows papal bull
grand pastures full of concrete hand thicken
in the breach. Gestures preach sanity among the unforgiven
ingots cradle hardscrabble telephone jacks babbling
electronic cattle over clothespins laundry ropes
of electric fences prodding words plod the ramp
make twist and turns of sensory deprivation
in think tanks of the misbegotten,
mooning the misconstrued with acts of public recency.
What four the weight? Who will carrion the freight
of calamity Jainists seeking the one true gear
among the four-in-the-floor of everyday nuance?

A natural transition to be sure,
full stockyards calling spin-dry weather remains.
To be scene the rubble bubbles to the rain
its vamp an endless variant doubling its space
scores in haste of chaste remnants across the field
just in case the music of precautionary eight
measures bar doors against the lumberjacks

invasion of the decidedly indecisive raging
derisive jumbles jumping off the syntactical ledge
into slay of grapefruit. Sally forth, they treasure
galleries of sonic utensils cusping the want-nots
whose sculleries brace the incipient evasion
with tactile embassies lowing at manure's invidious
plop, each drop a sacred moment in citric history,
sonic dystopias raging silent harmonies against
the date of an upright sty. How else to measure
their good fortune of button-down innuendo?

As others wish at water's bottom, so may
the rays string guilts strich by stitch against the weary
barely aware of the scary possibilities
their unconsciousness implodes, the mother lode of all
culinary products notwithstanding the lust of the many
for the wary pew. Insurgent rivers amass the flame,
diverge as same, divulge the crass differential
of the axis in secret fluids of worship
rite below the others poking through their wells.

Interlocking sweeps degrees made for rooming
to saintly bottoms wet with dessert. Cream
dreaming supplies protean gerbils savagery's last
protein screams serenity's ultimate secret: the diet
of post-histrionic surfaces angling sly traces
of nicotine, earth as a dangling eye races
against the nuts of bolting Upanishads.

## The Unquestioned Answer

have you ever

if so
                    then

if not

have you never

if when
                    or not

ask why the why cares

**Tide Untimed**

Effluvial in their imprecocity
waves heighten the censor's sartorial flux.
The crux of the martyr
transforms its arterial lightning
to juxtapose the senseless
with all due intensity.

The fever eclipses sons,
daughters leave their brood
of sullen photos on the back porch,
family portraits
of the Laws of Physics.

Trains mute insensate glory
in refrain. The nectar breeds its hold.
The lute sings cold electric suns below the sky.
Wonderment beholds
the opposed intent, upholds dissident persuasions
The influx of incident brightens.
Bold staves of silence
creed the rector's arterial ducts.

Its sartor regards us
as heightening cholesterol
with numinous magic at the sight
of prophetic's bulge.
The sentence divulges the other,
presumes its disregard and cards it at the door.
The brother stands at the ready photo op
inaugurates its pledge.

Bravely the catechism erupts
perspicacious in its hectored ruin
while squandered nations abut their heads
issuing disclaimers
of all subsequent knowledge.

Foregone delusions irrationed
the hooded sentinels withhold their thrust
against pencilled flayers intent.
The glossolalia of graphite
declaims its songs against the sky
where sentiments have no intrusions
but sediment's aggressive layering.

## Unfounding Rumors

clandestine murmurs augment the seal
of blood the stake whose uptakes resound
farflung the moment of addendum's truth
surrounding the tortured heal of wounding

redounds with utmost fervor
the myriad glisten of the lake
sounding the bottom's air

intensifies the rippling intent
of mussels standing in the breach of epaulets
configured with luminary's

disdain rustling coattails

in the red heart of NO EXIT signs

a passion only upstarts command

astride the heat of the paddling liver
the rakes berate the wound of insolence
insatiable in their hunger for the stable
ozone whose sound sings river's bed
while dreadlocks coil the purpose

for giving vapor bounds
under listening treasures the list
surrounds the flat key

the moment rebounds
to stretch the wretched film of elasticity
its instant measure

airs red intentions with all due dismay
to reveal the flapcoat's rarified absence

today with absinthe clocks

the rock unfolds its heel

walls feel its closing pressure

emboldening dead inventions

## Urban Dawns

Radio alarm clocks ring
the entire city. Entities arise,
birds cry truculent drivers.
Reverse pieties endure perverse
coagulations of a nation in turned moil.

Oil sings ballads. String saves
yarns from boring well. To cling
raves bring run to magnets distract
attraction's finest momentum.
Sting love's inert body with hasty

wishes paste waste devoid of sound
geometry. Startlings die in ale,
trails of ancient descent bent dry.
Their stinging flies duped fins again
whenever the mass of flailed failings

try yet again to bring.

**Weekends at the Lab**

penumbral Sundays unspent
the intuition of inertia's costly means
energy budgets

for the dissipation

of caterpillars

gardens unreached tend
toward the sabbatical especially
interfacing

with the animation

the will withheld

august emissaries protest
the assumption that all things being
equals a sun

stationed among cartoons

figures fill the accord

plants with animal mix
genetic engineering breeds its grain
intellect surfaces

its polyurethane trellis

still in its shadowed yield

## Widening the Gyros

never the twain
shall mark the meat
butchery
is its foregone sweep

racing against steak
the plummet cries

its pained shark
sweet to the touch
so much so that
the sty may live

unherald its coming
tuesday's armaggedon

weep for the massive
who know no bettor
or share the gambol

**Yet Another**

this time the line
shrapnel the time's effluvia
in porcine haste

no flavor to extract
distraction's comely bid
or center its off

limes leaves its pine
sent to the nearest customer
off the cusp

love greets its trilogy
with mirrored reflections
seeking same-

ness of difference
in secrets bulging divulgence
knickers thighs

convenient lies
telling truth directions
of repetition

## Outmoded Surrealistic Structure No. 1

'twas the night before Artaud
& all through the cat's lumbago
hotspur jackals evinced their semen
in vats of germinal concern

in her apocryphal tower Nadja weeps
*por nada en espanol*

navel juxtapositions eat fish
over the broken bred of Aragont poets
trifling with the truffles in their
fists posing over notes to be penned
in the cages on the backs of manuscript pages

Nadja weeps towers of *nada*
in her apocryphal *espanol, por* her

secretions delete all grief
numbered sequentially for their ruin
intrepid integers of formalistic pursuits
retread their horrible entities
raise the dead with automatic

weeps *en espanol por nada*
in her tower of apocryphal Nadja

over deletions intrinsic to bleeding
watches the Dali she cradles in her
melting watches a maternity of tabloid
pursuit consistent with the manifestoes
of Mayan glyphs riffing cliff-held artifacts

*por nada en* Nadja's *espanol*
her apocrypha weeps in tower

## Outmoded Surrealistic Structure No. 2

It all began in Ernst
when Dali Maximized Venus
in her breast drawer closet
or so Antoine are told

no man can expect head
from a Venus without one

limbic rage pursues its equivalent absence
in the lumbar regions where Pluto folds way
among the dungeons of the languid
and their primary interceptors

skepticism breeds its own content
in the guise of form

exhorted on a boys night out
gawkng down topless runways
featuring exotic plantains to go
bananas over light

strobing the play of darkness
the sculptress needs her sew

to darken the impenetrable delay
with facile nurturing of mothers' hooves
the stag parties its anticipation
ramming delayed gratification

its ramifications self-serving
the undeserving ramparts

leaps the turbaned sky
its crescent arc demands
restitution for prostitution
of past justices milking

in the bark tower
of the savage noman

## Outmoded Surrealistic Structure No. 3

Nepenthe the curmudgeon calls
bricks his backyard sticks prunes
into the tithes of asphalt

adventures of falling dentures
need not apply to all the carping winners
of atrophy gold on the white-haired

disco chest pursuing dudgeons
friskily betraying the fiscally fit
laying their investitures on the side

a privilege of orifice undaunted
by the bludgeon of oral monikers
physical in their nominative cases

of beer for picnics of plastic mustaches
cheering their own exhibit of their un-
conscious mastery of conquests

driven by trophy statues without arms
to keep abreast of while leering at
the fields leaping over their sheep

## Sonnet

the technocracy of uproarious glissando
perpetrates stories of glorious bliss and though
the missing protest perpetuates the ancient stories
through boring reckonings twist its fate

delight among the measured
knows no pleasured bounds of distention
speaking forensically of course
treasure demands its right to salvage

hulls wreck no glories nor blow gales
creaking masts intrinsically stale bread below
the hold of untold ballast seeks dimensions
beyond electrodes of distant enemies

bold crackles assert invidious silence
intent with tracks of insidious measure

## ABOUT THE AUTHOR

Vernon Frazer received his B.A. in English from the University of Connecticut. He has studied creative writing with Rex Warner, James Scully, and Brendan Galvin, string bass with Bertram Turetzky and music theory with Ran Blake.

Frazer's poetry and fiction have appeared in numerous magazines, as well as in book form. His non-fiction has appeared in *Poets & Writers*, the *Hartford Advocate* and the Hartford *Courant, Batteries Not Included, Coda, Cadence* and *Jazz Hot.*

A part-time bassist, Frazer fused poetry with music from 1988 to 1994 with the Maynard G. Krebs Memorial Ensemble, the Vernon Frazer Poetry Band and the Vernon Frazer-Thomas Chapin Duo. In addition to releasing three recordings, Frazer's poetry-music combos performed at the Nuyorican Poets Café and the Knitting Factory, as well as numerous other venues throughout the northeastern United States . In 1994, saxophonist Thomas Chapin commissioned "Put Your Quarter In and Watch the Chicken Dance" for his *Menagerie Dreams* CD. The piece later appeared on *THE JAZZ VOICE*, a CD compilation of vocalists and poets co-sponsored by the Knitting Factory and the *Village Voice.*

Frazer lives in East Hartford, Connecticut with his wife, Elaine Kass.

## ARTISTS STATEMENT

Throughout my writing I've explored the relationship between literature and music, particularly contemporary jazz in its most innovative forms.

If improvisation, the primary tool of jazz musicians, enables me to maintain a sense of freshness while I'm writing, revision allows me to smooth the rough edges inherent in improvisation while retaining a sense of spontaneity in the work.

My attempt to understand the free improvisation of Ornette Coleman, Cecil Taylor and many other noteworthy practitioners persuaded me that their idiom was, in a sense, as much a "literary" form as a musical form. The metric and harmonic freedom of free jazz matched the flow of free verse more than it did the structure of standard tunes, the basis of most modern jazz. My fusion of poetry with music rested on this understanding; I tailored the bass lines that guided the movement of the instrumentalist's improvisations to the poetic text. In effect, I applied the harmolodic theories of Ornette Coleman to the fusion of free verse and free improvisation.

*Demolition Fedora* explores poetry as a form of free improvisation, using sound and syntax in ways that defy conventional meaning, and the computer as an "instrument," much as the typewriter was for Charles Olson. The improvisational aspect of literary composition (and necessary revisions) involves fracturing conventional meaning with words that jar the reader/listener's ear toward a different perception. Sound takes precedence over sense.

Removing the poem's traditional intent to "mean" enhances its ability to "be," i.e., a perception in process open to the reader's interpretation, although I doubt that Archibald MacLeish would agree.